The Life & Times of Inigo McKenzie

Enough, Inigo, Enough

by Janet Doman
illustrated by Michael Armentrout

The Gentle Revolution Press ™
Towson, Maryland

This printing 2002
The Gentle Revolution Press™
810 Gleneagles Court, Suite 305
Towson, MD 21286 U.S.A.

Design and Direction: Phyllis Sherowitz Shenny

        Second Edition

Library of Congress Catalog in Publication Data
Armentrout, J. Michael
Doman, Janet J.

        Enough, Inigo, Enough

        1. Infants 2. Education, pre-school I. Title

ISBN: 1-59117-005-2

Printed in Hong Kong

My name is Inigo McKenzie.

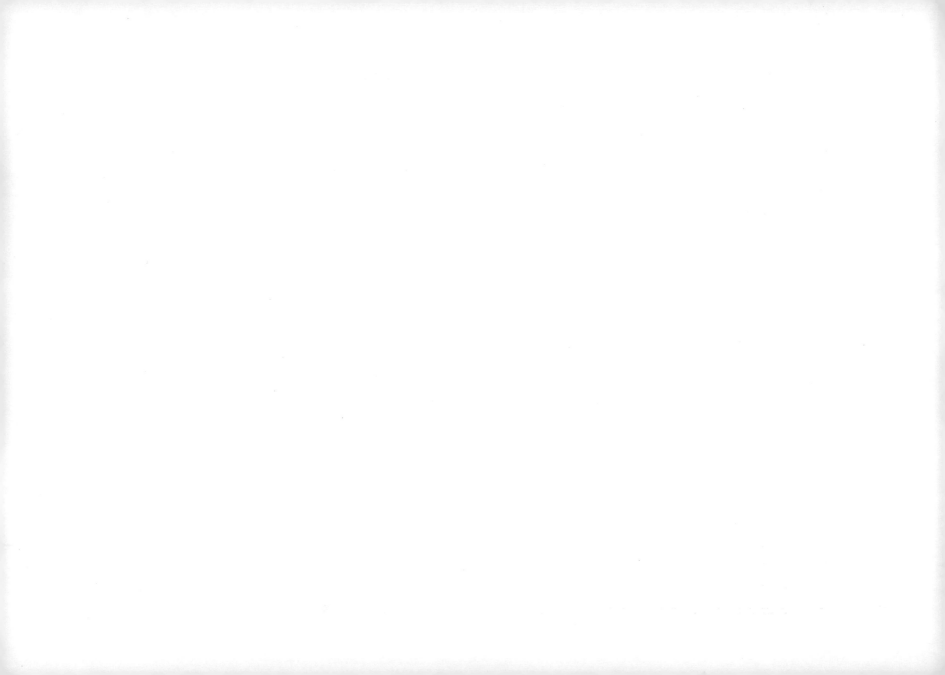

4

That is my dog
sleeping next to me.

His name is
Moonshine.

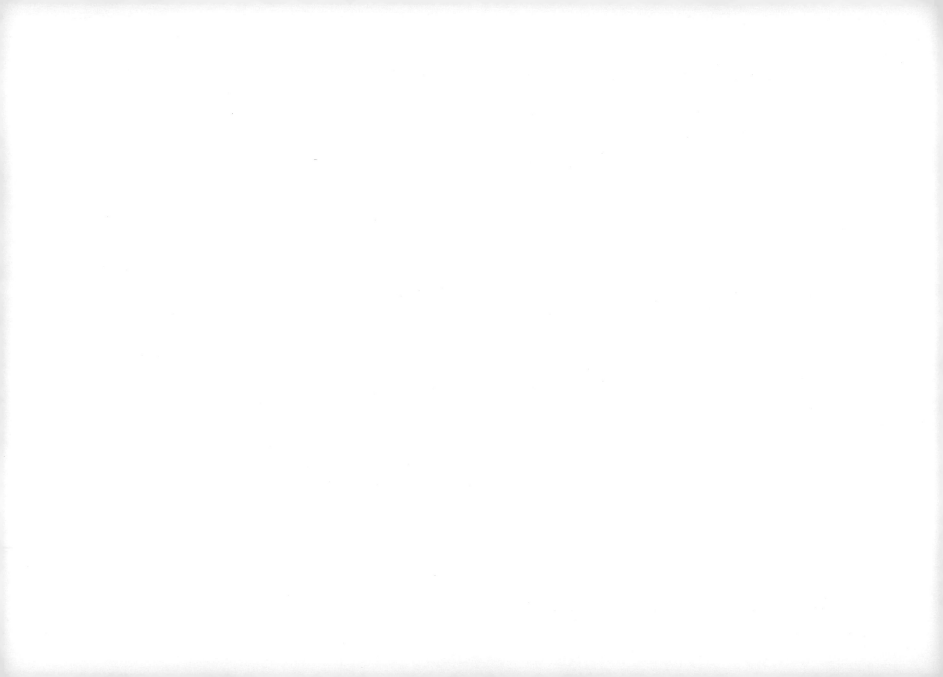

Here I am when I was two with my family.

A baby you say?

Look again.

I was little but strong.

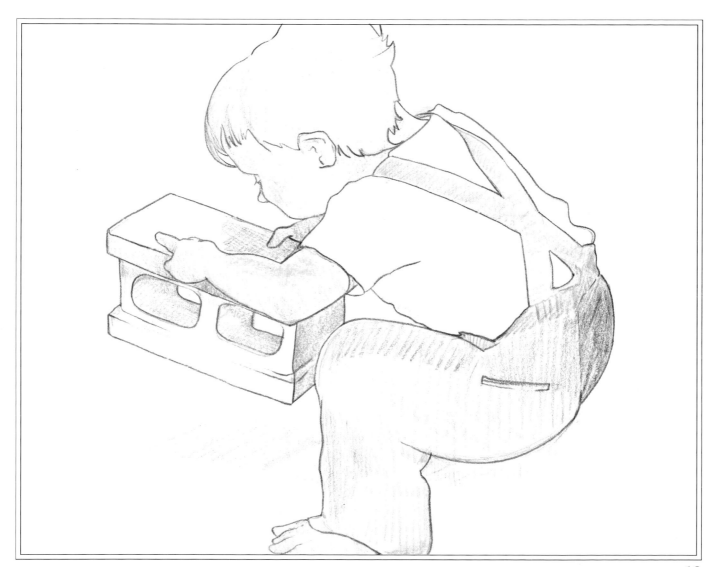

I liked climbing the refrigerator.

"Watch out for low flying bananas!"

My brother said,
"Enough, Inigo,
enough!"

I liked jumping on the bed

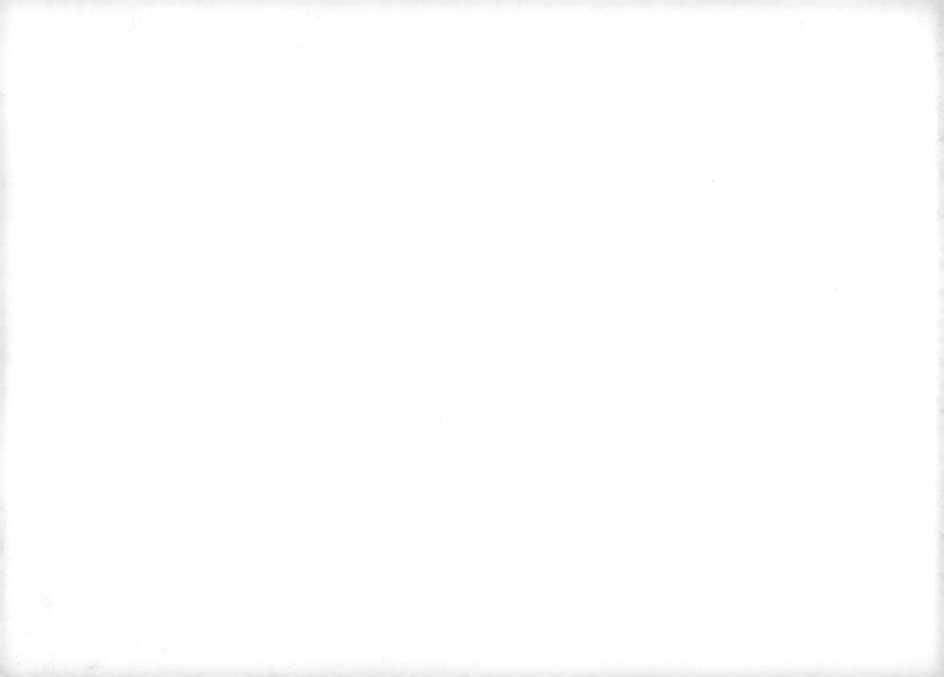

into my father's
arms.

My father said,
"Enough, Inigo,
enough!"

I liked swimming in the bathtub

blowing bubbles at
the hippopotami.

The hippos said,
"Enough, Inigo,
enough!"

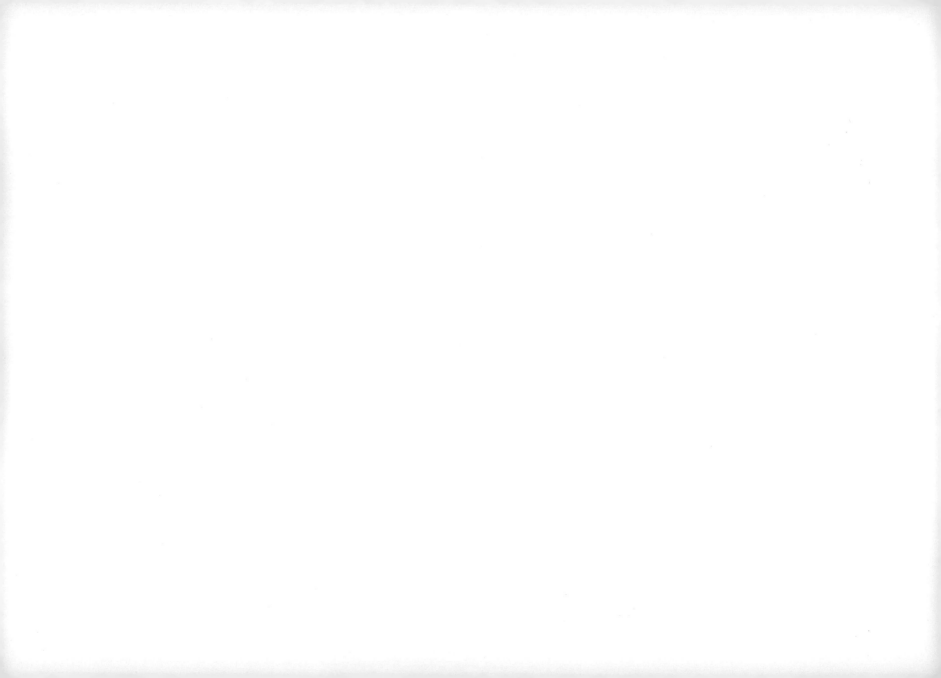

I was short in those days but I could eat!

I loved eating in my high chair;

carrots, oranges,
grapes, apples,
strawberries,
cherries, peaches...

My sister said,
"Enough, Inigo,
enough!"

I was tiny but funny.

I loved throwing spaghetti on the floor.

The spaghetti said,
"Basta, Inigo, basta!"

That means "Enough, Inigo, enough!" in Italian.

I was young but bright.

I knew a red truck from a blue truck.

I knew my right hand from my left hand.

And I certainly knew
"up" from "down!"

However I had some trouble tying my shoes.

Moonshine always said, "Arf, arf, arf!"

That means "Enough, Inigo, enough!"

I loved reading with
my mother best of all.

"Bellybutton" was my favorite!

And "nose" and "ear" and "elbow" and "teeth" and "finger" and "toes" and...

My mother sometimes said, "Enough, Inigo, enough!"

But I always said,
"Again, Mommy,
again!"

About the book

In 1963 the publication of the book *How To Teach Your Baby To Read* by Glenn Doman signaled the beginning of a revolution in the way children's books are written and designed. The first books designed to be read by two- and three-year-old children were written by Glenn Doman and illustrated by his fourteen year old daughter Janet. The story behind *Enough, Inigo, Enough* is really the story of The Institutes for the Achievement of Human Potential in Philadelphia.

The pioneering work of The Institutes was begun by its founder, Glenn Doman, prior to World War II. In 1945 Glenn resumed his work with brain-injured children which led to discoveries in child brain development that proved to be vital to well children, especially in the area of early reading.

Reading programs were designed and taught to the mothers of severely brain-injured children by The Institutes under the direction of Katie Doman, Glenn's wife. By the time *How To Teach Your Baby To Read* was published, it was common for two and three year old brain-injured children to be able to read and mothers of well children were also discovering that tiny well children could read too.

In 1974 a team of Institutes' staff were invited by the founder of SONY to teach English to Japanese mothers and children in Tokyo at the Early Development Association. When this team returned to Philadelphia two years later they established the first of the institutes to be devoted to teaching mothers of well children how to develop their tiny children intellectually, physically and socially.

In 1980 a demonstration school was established at The Institutes to show how the principles of child brain development can be used to create an effective and stimulating curriculum that is respectful of the enormous abilities of young children and to continue on with research in this area.

Shortly thereafter a one week course for mothers was begun. To this day mothers come to The Institutes from around the world to learn the principles of child brain development and to gain practical knowledge of how to use those principles to design their own home programs.

As the course became increasingly well known thousands of parents enrolled and afterward wanted to maintain a close relationship with The Institutes. An off-campus program was then designed which allowed the graduates of the one-week course (regardless of where they live) to enroll their children and receive professional guidance and teaching materials.

Today The Institutes' staff continue to research and develop new programs and materials and to teach parents of well and brain-injured children. Each year the staff sees thousands of parents and children in Philadelphia and at locations around the world.

The Life and Times of Inigo McKenzie Series is the first step toward making available to mothers around the world the hundreds of children's books written over the last quarter of a century. *Enough, Inigo, Enough* is the result of the vast experience of the entire Institutes' staff in teaching mothers and children and is intended to be used and enjoyed as part of the reading program outlined in Glenn Doman's books *How To Teach Your Baby To Read* and *How To Multiply Your Baby*'s Intelligence.

About the author

Janet Doman is the Director of The Institutes for the Achievement of Human Potential in Philadelphia, Pennsylvania.

Janet grew up at The Institutes and was pitching in to help brain-injured children by the time she was nine years old. She was directly involved in The Institutes' groundbreaking work in early reading. At fourteen she illustrated one of the first books ever published which was written and designed to be read by two and three year old children. These books were written by Glenn Doman.

After completing studies in zoology at the University of Hull in England and physical anthropology at the University of Pennsylvania. Janet devoted herself to teaching early reading programs to parents at The Institutes.

In 1974 she headed the team sent to Japan to teach English to mothers and babies at the Early Development Association in Tokyo.

The program created by this team was an immediate success. After two years she returned to the United States and helped to create the first institute of The Institutes to be devoted to teaching mothers of well children how to deveop their tiny children intellectually, physically and socially.

Recently Janet and her father have updated and revised Glenn's International best-selling books *How To Teach Your Baby To Read*, *How To Teach Your Baby Math* and *How to Multiply Your Baby*'s Intelligence. She co-authored *How To Give Your Baby Encyclopedic Knowledge*. The Life and Times of Inigo McKenzie Series is part of a larger project to make teaching materials which are consistent with The Institutes' philosophy available to mothers.

Janet spends most of her day nose-to-nose with "the best mothers in the world," helping them to discover the vast potential of their babies and their own potential as teachers.

About the illustrator

Michael Armentrout is an artist whose graphic work has been exhibited throughout the United States as well as Canada, France, Italy, Japan and Mexico.

More Information About
How To Teach Your Child

How To Teach Your Baby Catalogs:
    The Gentle Revolution Catalog
    The Programs of The Institutes

Books:
    How To Teach Your Baby To Read
    How To Teach Your Baby Math
    How To Multiply Your Baby's Intelligence
    How To Give Your Baby Encyclopedic Knowledge
    How To Teach Your Baby To Be Physically Superb
    What To Do About Your Brain-Injured Child

Materials:
    How To Teach Your Baby To Read™ Kits
    How To Teach Your Baby Math™ Kits
    How To Multiply Your Baby's Intelligence® Kits

Children's Books:
    The Life & Times of Inigo McKenzie
    Nose Is Not Toes

Courses:
    How To Multiply Your Baby's Intelligence® Course
    What To Do About Your Brain-Injured Child® Course

For course and program information, please contact:
    The Institutes for the Achievement of Human Potential®
    8801 Stenton Avenue
    Wyndmoor, PA 19038 USA
    www.iahp.org
    PHONE: 215-233-2050
    FAX: 215-233-3940

For books and teaching materials, please contact:
    The Gentle Revolution Press
    810 Gleneagles Court, Suite 305
    Towson, MD 21286 USA
    www.gentlerevolution.com
    TOLL-FREE PHONE: 866-250-BABY
    FAX: 410-337-3544